Idealist Dreams: How I Learned to Plan as an INFP

Arcadia Page

Published by Arcadia Page, 2018.

IDEALIST DREAMS: HOW I LEARNED TO PLAN AS AN INFP

First edition. December 25, 2018.

ISBN: 979-8201549053

Written by Arcadia Page.

Table of Contents

Special thanks to my husband, who put up with me as I spent money and unusual amounts of time testing out planners and notebooks until I found what works for me.

Note from the Author

When I first published this little book in December of 2018, I knew that it covered the best of what I knew at the time. However, I had a hunch that there would be more for me to learn, try, and apply that would make the journey of figuring out how to map out my time and projects better.

Sure enough, I came across a few new methods that made planning more powerful for me. I have updated this book with those methods.

Much of this book now reflects my deeper understanding of "Big Picture Thinking." It has become an overused term in many ways, but as an INFP, I found that understanding this has been the key to plotting my time and projects in a way that's not only simple but effective.

My new understanding of this concept inspired me to reorganize this book. The order of this book has been heavily influenced by the website for the Australian National University[1], but for my purposes, it's a perfect fit. This book now goes from the widest view, which is Understanding Yourself, to the smallest detail which is Managing Tasks. This order also maps well with the INFP function stack.

The first chapter, **Understanding Yourself**, fits with the INFP's primary use of introverted feeling. The **Big Picture Planning** chapter works the INFP's secondary function, extroverted intuition. **Establishing a Routine** involves using the tertiary function of introverted sensing. Then finally the last two chapters, **Completing Tasks** and **Managing Your Day** align with inferior extroverted thinking.

The benefit of ordering the chapters this way is that what you're fantastic at is covered first, giving you the strength to handle the weaker areas of

---

1. https://www.anu.edu.au/students/academic-skills/study-skills/time-management/
   big-picture-planning

introverted sensing and extroverted thinking near the end. The flow of this updated book is more intuitive.

If you're not familiar with functions, don't worry. You don't need to fully understand them to use this book. But if you're curious and would like to learn more about functions, I suggest starting with **The 8 Functions at Personality Junkie**[2] and the post **How Each Cognitive Function Manifests Based On Its Position In Your Stacking** by Heidi Priebe at Thought Catalog[3].

Also in this book I introduce a touch of Socionics Theory. Socionics is considered a different system from Myers-Briggs, but I've gained some insights from the Socionics theory that have been helpful with getting a more rounded view of my inner workings. True, there is some argument over Socionics versus Myer-Briggs, but my feelings are that if a system offers useful information, it's worth considering deeply. I was introduced to Socionics via the post **The Five Differences Between Socionics and Myers-Briggs** by Johaness Karlsson at Psychology Junkie[4], and I found it fascinating.

In updating this book, I also focused on simplifying and streamlining. I wanted this information to be as straightforward and useful as possible. Along with that, I've added some new illustrations.

I know that is a bit much for an update, but I didn't want there to be an inferior version of my book floating out there as a 1st edition. I wanted this edition to be the best. So I apologize for any lost highlights and bookmarks due to this update. Maybe you'll come to forgive me...

---

2. https://personalityjunkie.com/myers-briggs-functions-inferior-function/

3. https://thoughtcatalog.com/heidi-priebe/2015/12/how-each-cognitive-function-manifests-based-on-its-position-in-your-stacking/

4. https://www.psychologyjunkie.com/2019/04/20/the-five-differences-between-socionics-and-myers-briggs/

My hope is that this book will help you discover your own method for reaching your idealist dreams.

Understanding Yourself

Talking and laughing relatives crammed into my aunt's modest double-wide. Her home had the temporary mixed fragrance of mac and cheese and fried seafood. Everyone lined up for food—all of my cousins ages two to thirty, Mom, Dad, aunts and uncles. My aunt who invited us swatted away an unwelcome fly that slipped in due to my younger cousins constantly running in and out the front door.

After filling my foam plate, I sat on the floor at the coffee table in the living room since there was nowhere else to sit. My aunts and uncles reclined on the surrounding sofa, taking in a basketball game that blared from the TV. My older cousins laughed loudly as they sat in a corner playing Spades, a game I've played a few times but have little interest in. The sounds of ten different conversations and the smells of ten different foods surrounded me, and I was okay with it. Until I wasn't.

After eating, I retreated to the bedroom a female cousin of mine gave up so I could have my own room to stay in while my family visited. She had mounted a skateboard on a wall and used the wheels to organize her necklaces. A messy pile of music magazines lay in a box next to the bed. As I pulled a sketchbook out of my bag to enjoy some private drawing time, there was a knock on the door. I opened it.

My mom stood there.

"Come back out and spend some time with your family," she said.

My hands gripped my sketchbook, crinkling the paper.

"I don't want to."

I regretted those words as soon as I said them, but I couldn't bring myself to lie either.

My mom's smiled flat-lined. "We traveled all the way here to see them. You better get back out there," she said.

I didn't understand why at the time, but tears started rolling down my face.

"I hate it here," I said.

However, Mom would not take "no" for an answer. "You get back out there," she repeated. An ultimatum.

So sure enough, I washed my face and got back out there, because I didn't want to face her anger. Yet, I was absolutely miserable. This is what played out every time I visited my Mom's family from the time I was fifteen until my early twenties.

As I look back, I now understand that I didn't hate being around my family. Instead, that chaotic environment pushed me into a double breakdown. I was having an introvert meltdown and a HSP meltdown simultaneously. However, the understanding I have today could have saved me and my mom from showing our worst selves over and over.

If I knew what I know now, I would have retreated from that situation long before I had crossed the point of no return. And if my mom had come looking for me, I would have had the presence of mind to say, "Mom, I'm feeling tired and overwhelmed right now. Just give me a moment to myself, and then I'll spend some more time with everyone."

To me this life experience is an enduring example of how not knowing what you're made of and not knowing how to express and work with that, can cause unnecessary problems. A lot of pain has disappeared from my life by knowing my optimal modes of functioning as an HSP and INFP. Even more pain was reduced when I learned that I have multiple overexcitabilities as well. These realizations have impacted how I plan my day and my future.

By knowing who you are and the way you process information as an INFP and as an individual, you will remove much of the pain from the process of planning your day and reaching your life goals.

FiNeSiTe

If you're an INFP, have you ever felt like you can't get things done because it's hard to stick to anything? Or like having to a to-do list is so suffocating that you would rather not have one, yet the idea of having a method of accomplishing things is still strangely appealing?

Being an INFP means being introverted, intuitive, and always looking for possibilities in the world. We use introverted feeling to pick out what's meaningful to us, and extroverted intuition connects what we view as valuable and not valuable, creating a web of information in our minds.

Personality types who use extroverted intuition are known for their multiplying ideas. The challenge of using extroverted intuition is that for anything to be accomplished with it, the energy from it needs to be handled with skill. I've found one way to do that is by having a basic planning method.

I don't know how many times I've gone to the store and picked out for myself a planner that I thought would change everything. *This year, I'm going to get it right*, I would think to myself. One or two months after using my shiny new planner, I would find that the excitement has worn off, and by the end of the year I'm throwing out another less than half-used planner.

The reason why traditional methods of planning don't work for me is because as an INFP, it's hard to stick to routines. Organization lore says that you're supposed to check your planner every morning. Sometimes I do. Sometimes I don't. But I do know that when I don't look at my planner for months, it becomes useless.

Another thing about being an INFP and planning is the influence of the inferior function, **extroverted thinking**. If you're new to the concept of functions, *Was That Really Me?* by Naomi Quenk explains in a clear, easy to understand way how functions work for each MBTI type. She also highlights how the inferior function holds a certain attractiveness.

For INFPs, although completely giving in to extroverted thinking can lead to the dark side, we are attracted to having structure in our lives and getting things done. Although we are not the most proficient at those things, we kind of desire them.

I love my introverted feeling and extroverted intuition, but it is challenging having introverted sensing and extroverted thinking as my lower two functions.

Sensing and extroverted thinking includes the concepts of:

- Sticking to a routine

- Getting as many tasks done as possible each day

- Keeping to a schedule

- Keeping an orderly environment

All traditional planning skills are my weak spots.

At one time I was using an hour by hour scheduler, and for two months, I was enjoying it. However, by the third month, I noticed that I was just writing the same stuff day after day. I was starting to get frustrated because it seemed like my free time kept getting eaten by more stuff to do. By month four I was like, "Forget this scheduling stuff. I'll do things when I want to!"

Looking back, I realize that hourly scheduling may not be the best for someone whose ideas and thoughts multiply by nature. When I set aside a block of free time and said, "I will put no tasks in this time frame" when that time came around, I found myself unsatisfied because I felt like working during my "free time." Conversely, I often felt like relaxing and doing nothing during my scheduled "project times." My mind works on its own cycle without a consistent rhythm. Trying to adjust my schedule to my whims was a pain because what I felt like doing was unpredictable. I can't schedule my feelings.

However, with a lot of experimenting, I was able to find some planning tips that worked for me. I hope some of these tips will help other INFPs find a way to plan that fits their idea growing, open-ended way of thinking.

Since this book will engage your inferior extroverted thinking, I suggest that you take your time going through it, especially as you get to the last three chapters.

Dig into Your Motives

In the Socionics personality theory, INFPs fall into the Yielding category, which says something interesting about how INFPs view time. Personality types in the Yielding category tend to hold tightly to their resources, mainly time and money, and are generous with their ideas and creativity. The point is that time is a precious resource to INFPs. Many of us fear wasting it or not using it in a way that allows us to be our best selves.

In fact, it was this fear that motivated me to dig deeply into planning. After getting married, I found that I had to juggle work, household stuff, time with friends, time with my family, time with my husband's family, and time I needed for myself. I had the sensation of being whisked along through life like a speck of dust being driven by a broom. Yes, I need to buy groceries, but what about my writing? What about my art? Will I ever have time to do anything meaningful again? The avalanche of mundane tasks was overwhelming. I fell into depression because little of what I did every day felt meaningful.

Time is precious. I knew I needed to use it better.

That was my reason for starting my planning journey.

What is your reason for wanting to plan better? Why? Take five minutes to write about it.

Acknowledge Planning Failures

Early in my planning journey, I bought a popular brand of planner. Large, colorful, with disc-rings marked by a huge heart-shaped punch out, I was sure this planner would match my planning needs. Along with it came a fantastic selection of cute and motivational stickers that encouraged me to *Seize the Day* and be a *Girlboss*. Plus, it was the first time I had ever seen a planner that would allow me to divide my day into morning, noon, and evening, instead of giving me a threatening time-table to fit my tasks into.

My life with this planner started out happily enough, but overtime—I used it less and less. I've always been intrigued by the idea of making my own printables for my planner. However, this planner was not a standard size. If I wanted to make printables, I would have to cut the pages down and make a bunch of paper waste. That process didn't sit well with me.

I also found that adding pages of topical notes to this planner in a way that made sense to me was not happening. In less than six months our relationship came to an end. I know for some people, this is the perfect planner. It may even be the perfect planner for you. Unfortunately, it didn't fit me.

I decided that maybe what I needed was more freedom for my plans and notes. I came across the Bullet Journal and started doing that instead. I Bullet Journalled for a long time off and on. It was this awkward dance of almost perfection. With handling my notes and tasks, this system was perfection. When it came to a wider view of time, I had difficulties adding the way I thought into the notebook.

The name-brand planner had too much structure, even locking me into an odd size of paper. On the other hand, the Bullet Journal gave me too little structure, although I enjoyed the creativity of it, and I mention it often in this book with love.

So those are my planning failures.

What planning failures have you had? Why do you think those failures happened?

List what went wrong, and then write what you think could have been done to overcome those problems.

Do What Works

The most organized I've ever been with my time was when I was in middle school and high school. My 6th grade homeroom teacher passed out the school issued planners to the class. The cover was mostly plain white with the school's blue lightning bolt logo emblazoned on it. The inside cover had lines for my name and teacher in case I lost it.

The inner layout was basic. There was a monthly calendar, perfect for keeping track of due dates. Then there was a weekly calendar designed for keeping track of my assignments for each class. It wasn't fancy or encouraged me to track my habits or do daily gratitude—but it did its main job well. It was the most effective planner I ever had.

I never missed a due date and all my assignments were turned in on time throughout middle school. At the start, my teachers would check in on me to make sure I was using the planner—the teachers did that with everyone. But once I was in the habit of filling it out and I was doing well with my classes, there was no reason for them to check anymore.

In high school I didn't have a class planner, but I already had a habit of putting due dates on a calendar and keeping a task list of assignments for each class. The basic skills for planning stuck with me, but when adult life free of school came, I had to learn how to upgrade my planning, and that learning curve has been steep.

Think back to your most successful planning experience (Planning a vacation or a party counts too). What do you think made that experience successful? What could you do to repeat that?

Throughout this book I'll be sharing a lot of things that I've found helpful and got me going in the right direction with the way I plan my time. But if you have something that you currently use that's working for you, don't change it! This book is just a palette of planning techniques. I'm simply sharing what I've found to be helpful, and what worked for me may or may not work for you.

Understand What You Already Have and Enjoy

After graduating from college and getting married, I found myself deluged with responsibilities. In my life things usually fall into two categories: What I have to do and what I enjoy doing.

I have to go to work. I have to buy groceries. I have to pay rent.

I've also found it helpful to list items that I already have that I consider necessities.

Notebooks. Pens. A computer.

Take a moment and write a list of necessities and the things you have to do to get through life.

Don't feel embarrassed to add things like, "I have to drink coffee" or "I have to read books," if those are things you feel you need to function daily.

Then there are things that I enjoy.

I enjoy reading, music, friends, family, writing, etc...

Make a list of what you enjoy. Think about how you typically like to spend your time and money.

Don't worry if some of the same things on your Enjoy list are on your Have list. When what you enjoy overlaps with what you have, those items are easier to take care of.

As for the activities on your Have list that don't overlap with what you enjoy:

Is there a way to simplify them so they take less time and energy? Can you add an element of something you enjoy to make them easier?

For example, you may enjoy a cup of tea, but doing taxes—not so much. Could drinking tea while doing taxes make that task a little more bearable?

By reducing the time, effort, and emotional stress of the things on your Have list, you will not only have more time to spend on what you enjoy, but you'll get things done at the same time.

Introducing these two lists in a chapter about understanding yourself may seem a bit strange. However, having a clear view of what you already have in your life and what you enjoy helps with understanding what you're working with, internally and externally. Plus, both lists provide a quick overview of what is important to you.

Planning is all about setting priorities, so knowing what's important to you is the first place to start.

Big Picture Planning

Another story idea hit me. I didn't know the title yet, but I knew that I wanted my story to be about a girl who possessed special powers that belonged to a limited number of people. I wanted romance, adventure, and personal angst. And maybe a cool bad guy. Yesss....

The real problems began when I started thinking about how to get there. Did I want this story to be told in comic form or in prose? How was I going to approach each chapter? What is the more detailed plot?

Many INFPs are "Big Picture" thinkers. Unfortunately, this is one of those terms that's thrown around so much, it's easy to forget what that even means.

Big Picture Thinking is a thinking style that focuses on the larger aims of a goal instead of the specific steps of how to get there. It's like being a fashion designer who wants to create a pair of pants that's comfortable, unique and affordable, but hasn't taken the time to figure out the details of what fabric is needed, how long it will take to make the pants, will it have an elastic waist band or a zipper enclosure, etc...

The focus is on the intentions of a project or goal, not the steps and details of getting there. Often, big picture thinkers discover the steps to achieving their goals as they go.

Another thing is that in general, INFPs tend to mentally and emotionally mesh with projects. Some personality types are totally fine with setting aside weekends to work on their projects. I've found that as an INFP, having a weekend only schedule can lead to forgetting about the project altogether, making little progress, or losing motivation. Since we are enmeshed with the process, good things happen when we make reaching our goals part of our daily lifestyle.

Being inside of the process is a gift because there's the joy of being motivated by the internal experience of reaching something we want.

To make big picture planning do the most work for me, I start with my intentions for a project and then break those down into smaller tasks that I can integrate into my daily lifestyle.

One resource I've found helpful with learning how to do this is **Design the Life You Love** by Ayse Birsel. If you want to learn more about deconstructing and reconstructing concepts to create something new, it's definitely a book to look into. Here I'm going to share how to use mind-mapping to break a goal into smaller steps.

I have used mind-mapping in the past and found it to be useless. However, thanks to Birsel's book, I learned that the problem was with how I approached mind-mapping. When I switched from using this technique to generate ideas to using it to define big picture goals better, it became more effective.

So first, write a list of projects and goals you would like to achieve. Write all of them.

Then grab another blank piece of paper or a journal. **In the center of the page, write one goal or project from your list.**

Here's one of mine as an example:

Read More Books

After writing your goal, think of a few things you hope to achieve by reaching it. **What are your intentions? If it's a project, what do you want the results to be?**

I listed three intentions for this goal to keep things simple, but you can add as many as you need. Once you've noted what qualities of the goal or project that are important to you, it's time to break them down into actions. For example, with the Reading More Books mind-map, I could ask myself, "How can I read more fiction?"

Then I divide that up into things I can try to read more fiction.

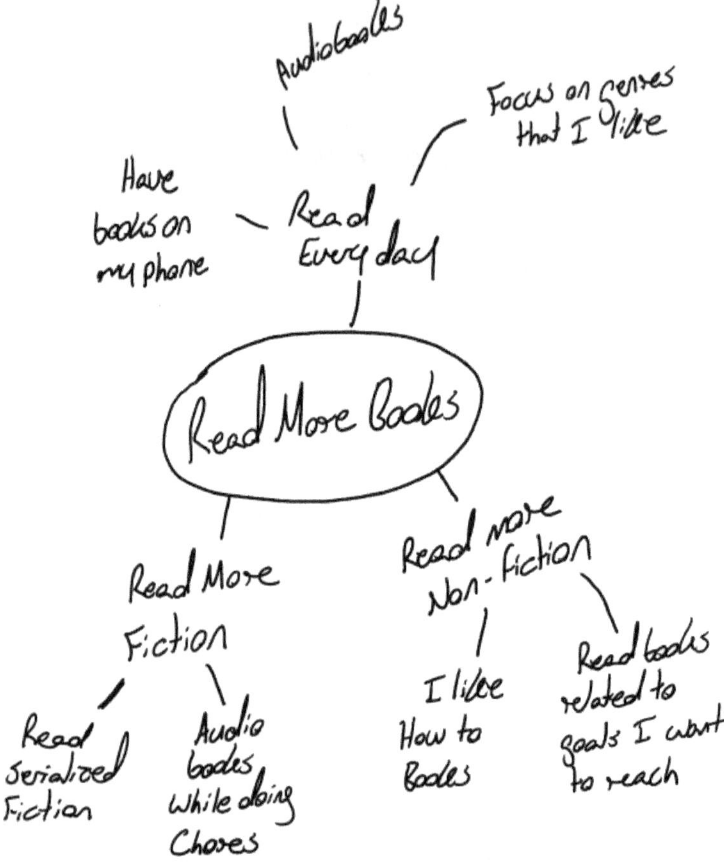

Intentions for goals can be a little different from intentions for projects. This mind-map for a sewing project is a good example:

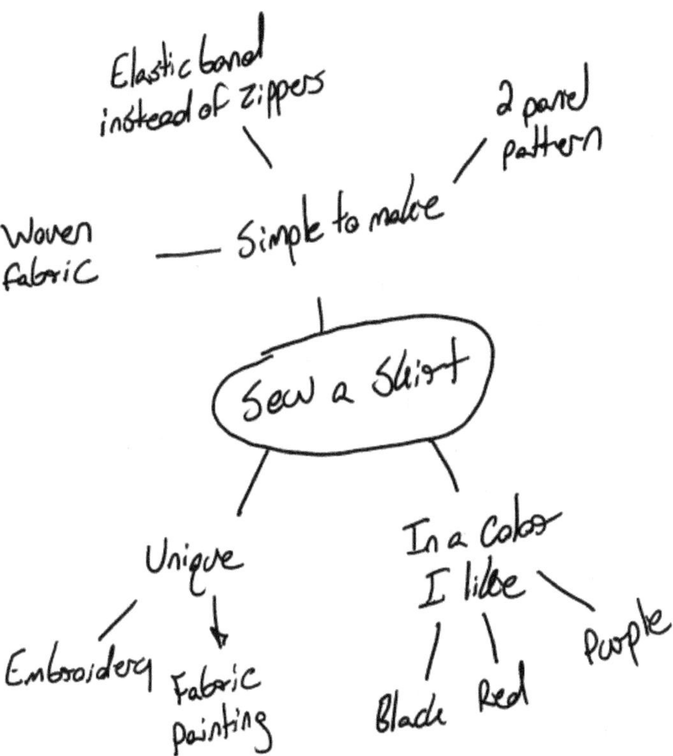

I wanted the result to be in a color I liked. So I asked myself, "What colors do I like?" I also asked myself questions like, "What is my definition of a simple skirt?" and "What would a unique skirt have?"

The outermost items of the mind-map are the basic ingredients you need to reach your goals.

For example, the ingredients for the skirt I wanted to create are:

- An elastic band.

- Woven fabric in red, black or purple.

- A two panel skirt pattern.

- Embroidery floss or fabric paint to add that unique touch.

Now that I know the details of what I need, there are four more questions I need to answer.

1. Do I need to gain more knowledge to achieve the intentions I have for this goal?
2. When would I like to finish this? (An etched in stone due date isn't necessary. Usually I find that deciding to try to finish something by the end of the month, within the next six months, or any other monthly time table, is good enough.)
3. Is there a way I can make this goal part of my lifestyle and work on it a little every day?
4. What do I need to do first?

Running with the sewing example, if I wanted this project to meet my intentions, at some point I would need to learn about fabric painting techniques, since I know little about that.

I could plan to finish this project before the end of the month, and set aside 15 minutes a day to work on it—from ordering fabric online to actually sewing it.

The first thing I would need to do is find a two panel skirt pattern. Then before buying the fabric, I would want to research fabric painting, because if I decide to go with that method, it could impact the fabric I buy.

If you find that a little research is necessary for a project, see if you could start the project anyways without that information. Sometimes research can become a form of procrastination. As you go, you may find that you didn't need that information after all. If you do need the research, you can look it up when you need it. This won't be an option for every project, but if you can, try getting started first and see how things come together.

If you have a complicated goal, you may find extra clarity by writing your ingredients in a chronological list. Then it can serve as your map (or you could try drawing an actual map for your project. That would be interesting...). You can cross off each item as it's completed.

Stacking Time

In the last section I mentioned working on a project a little every day. However, it may be difficult to figure out how much time every day works for you. 10 minutes? 20 minutes? 30?

To get a feel of how much project time you can handle daily, try starting with 5 to 10 minutes a day for a week. Stick to that time and do not go over it, even if you want to. View that extra energy as motivation to get back to it tomorrow. At the end of the week, take note of how you feel. Do you feel like you could do more? If so, add two minutes and stick to that for the next week. Every week add one or two more minutes until you find the amount of time that sits perfectly with you.

The same can apply to setting how long you plan to work on a project. Start with planning to work on a project for a week. At the end of the week gauge how you feel. Do you still have energy to work on it? If so, add another week. If you find yourself feeling bored, take a break from it for a week (maybe work on a different project) and then come back to it.

When you come back to it, has your energy returned? If so, that means you needed the break. If your energy doesn't return, you may need to reevaluate your level of interest in the project.

Do not underestimate the power of doing small actions every day to reach your goals. In the book **1000 Ideas by 100 Manga Artists** by Christian Campos, artist Akiko Matsuo says, "The quick route to success is to do creative activities steadily every day."

For more advice about working little and often, I also would highly recommend reading the free ebook, **Sustainable Creativity** by Michael Nobbs.

Dealing with Setbacks

Plans are rarely perfect. You may need to learn more about your project than you originally thought. Sometimes an extra step in the process appears out of nowhere. That's okay. As an INFP, you are equipped with extroverted intuition, which is a tool that enables you to quickly discover solutions in the outside world and improve as you go.

When I run into problems, I usually find answers by reading up on what others who have faced similar problems do or by giving my brain a break and allowing my subconscious to work on it. I rest my mind by washing dishes, wandering outside, showering, or napping. Often insights come to me while I'm taking a moment to sit around and stare into space.

When dealing with lack of focus, I've found it helpful to free-write or do breathing exercises for five to ten minutes before starting a project.

In general, I don't force myself to focus. If I can't focus on something, there is usually a good reason for it. Either I need to take a break and come back to it later, or it's something that's not aligned with what I need at the moment.

So, when you're having problems focusing, it could be that the current activity is not aligned with your needs, and some adjustments may need to be made. Try to do the activity at another time, at another place, or try out an alternative method of accomplishing the same thing.

Sometimes the biggest setback is life getting in the way. With some projects I've found myself battling lack of time, illness, or an overall lack of confidence. Taking the time to notice what those roadblocks are and pairing them with something enjoyable helps.

Do you enjoy something that can help you to overcome obstacles? Look at the Enjoy list you created earlier for inspiration.

Here are some ways I've paired up difficult tasks with things I enjoy:

- When I don't feel like writing, I write outside in nature with a cup of coffee.

- I listen to music and sew at the same time.

- I do chores while listening to entertaining audiobooks.

- I draw comics in bed.

Come up with whatever creative pairs you can. Then try to fit those pairs into your daily life so that you can make constant progress towards your goals.

Establishing a Routine

"If I could just focus and stick to it, I could accomplish so much more."

Extroverted Intuition seeks novelty. Routines are the opposite of that and involve our tertiary function of introverted sensing. As a result, routines can be hard for INFPs to maintain. I can't seem to keep up with cleaning day, grocery shopping day, and so on, but routines aren't entirely out of my reach.

Every morning I start my day with a cup of tea. After that point anything can happen. My morning routine has gone from breakfast-tea-journaling to breakfast-tea-exercise to tea-breakfast-deep breathing. The thing is, only two things on that list are routine: Tea and breakfast. And both of those can change. I can have different flavors of tea and kinds of breakfast meals. There is variety in this routine.

The best thing about having a routine is that it reduces decision fatigue and overwhelm. I don't have to try to decide when I want to journal or work on a project. Time is already built into my life for those things.

When it comes to creating my own personal routines, here are some techniques that I've found helpful:

The Not-So-Routine Routine

Pick one simple thing that you enjoy doing. Keep the thing you pick generalized. For example, reading is a good activity to start with because there's a wide variety of books. Then plan to do that activity after a meal, taking a shower, or something else that you've already had a habit of doing every day. So, let's say after dinner you will take 10 minutes to read.

Stick with that until it's something you routinely do. Allow at least two weeks to month. After you get that down, try to add something else. Like

"After dinner, I'll read a book for 10 minutes and then take 10 minutes to clean."Test that out and see how long you stick with it. If you get tired of it, swap cleaning with something else. You can go from dinner-read-clean to dinner-read-exercise to dinner-read-journal or you can swap the order of those things. The trick is to keep one or two things consistent and to anchor the routine to something that you already do regularly.

A Limited Time Routine

Another way to get things done on a somewhat routine basis is to set time limits on how long you plan to stick to it. In the past I've found success in planning to write every day for two weeks or cleaning the kitchen regularly for a month. After the time is up, I revert to my naturally haphazard ways. Routines are easy to keep for a short time.

Automatic Routines

Take full advantage of technology! Set as many routine tasks to happen automatically (bill pay, for example) as possible. There are also many online retailers who offer subscriptions for products that are purchased on a regular basis. If you keep forgetting to buy the toilet tissue, set an online subscription for it so it can be delivered to your house regularly. Don't take on more routine tasks than you need to.

Project Rituals

Before starting a project, you may want to put in place a routine that will help you focus. I've learned that this type of routine does not have to be long or complicated, and it varies by individual. In the past, I've tried tidying my studio before getting to work. That's a good fit for many artists, but not me. I don't find clutter in my room distracting, so doing that before working eventually felt like a waste of time.

Now what I do is close all of the open windows on my laptop except for what I'm working on, and I close the door to my room. Once I do that, I know I'm ready to focus. That is my ritual.

For projects, find a simple way that you can minimize distractions or prepare yourself before you start working. Do it every time before you start and eventually it will become a cue to your mind to focus.

Also what you do after session may be just as important as what you do before. Rewarding myself after finishing a project session gives me a ton of motivation to come back to my project again tomorrow. It's best if rewards are kept simple. I enjoy a cup of tea and a square of dark chocolate. Napping and spending time out in nature are also on my list.

To boost your motivation to be creative daily, make a list of inexpensive things that you could pamper yourself with after finishing a work session on your project.

And Don't Forget About Introverted Feeling...

Have you ever worked on a project that became so mesmerizing, you worked on it day after day without fail for an extended amount of time? That's not only flow, but also introverted feeling at work. Understanding introverted feeling and being aware of what lines up with your personal values can help with deciding what things should be made into a routine. If you're having problems sticking to something, it could be that it's not lining up with introverted feeling. Ask yourself, "What is the most interesting thing about this project? Is what I'm doing meaningful to me?"

I find that when I have a goal that lines up with my introverted feeling, I don't have to work hard to create a routine to get it done.

For more about introverted feeling, check out my blog post, Life as an
Introverted Feeling User[1].

---

1. http://www.arcadiapage.com/2018/03/life-as-introverted-feeling-user.html

Managing Your Day

Several months ago, I was doing some IT work on a coworker's computer. While I was waiting for software to install, I was mesmerized by the calendar on her wall. It wasn't the photography on it that captured my interest, although I enjoy pictures of nature and mountains. What struck me about her calendar is that, although it was a basic wall calendar, she had her entire week clearly laid out on it.

I realized that planning for the day or the week does not have to be complicated.

Step 1: Have a Calendar

Calendars are a must have to keep track of future events, due dates, and goals. Having a large monthly wall calendar is a good start, and it's the simplest solution.

What are the time sensitive items in your life right now? Are there due dates for bills or library books? Are there any future events coming up that you don't want to miss?

Take a moment to write down as many of those that come to mind.

Then get a calendar, and copy what's on your list to it. Also mark project related routines on the calendar as well.

For now, let's use the calendar mainly for time sensitive events and tasks. If you don't have a definite date for it, don't add it to the calendar. More general tasks will be handled in the next chapter.

Thoughts on Using a Wall Calendar

Did you know that you could use a wall calendar to schedule? I had no idea that it could be used that way, until my coworker's calendar taught me better.

- Things that happen in the morning are written at the top of the box for the day.

- Things that happen mid-day are written in the middle.

- Evening events are written at the bottom.

- If something has a more specific time, write the time next to it.

Scheduling, done.

Although I was in love with this method, I was so used to writing stuff where ever I wanted, that it was a little difficult at first. However once I started visualizing the vertical line of each day as a mini-timeline, this started to work for me.

With monthly calendars I've noticed that the more space there is to write (the bigger the boxes of the monthly calendar) the more likely having a monthly calendar alone will be fine. The less space, the more likely another medium (such as a weekly planner or BuJo) will be needed for details.

Speaking of Paper Planners...

If a more portable paper solution is needed, try a planner. One thing about planners is that they usually have two types of calendars: Monthly and Weekly. Some planners only have one, many have both. Monthly is the typical 30/31 days at a glance. Weekly is a layout that shows all seven days of the week on one or two pages.

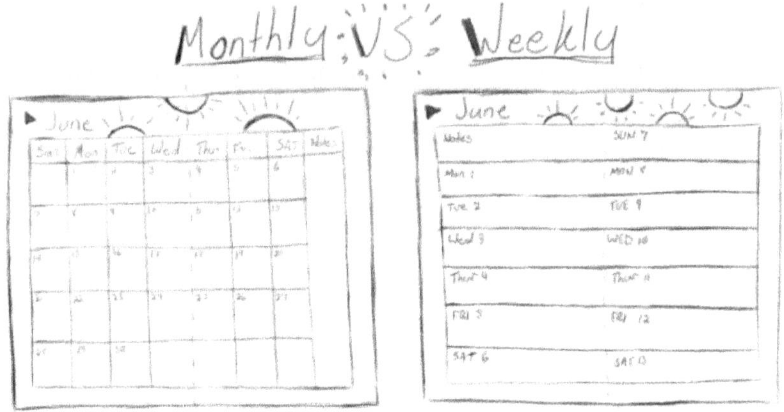

If you're using a monthly and weekly layout at the same time, see how things work if you use the monthly calendar for event names only and then use the weekly calendar for the details.

Extra Tips for Paper Planner Users

Unfortunately, planners fail to work when they're not looked at.

The best time to look at a planner is in the morning before the start of the day or in the evening at the end of the day. Doing this consistently can be challenging, but here are a few tips you can try to make it happen:

- Set an alarm or make a reminder to check your planner.

- Check your planner around mealtimes.

- Use a large planner and lay it out somewhere visible, like on a table.

Checking my planner at meal times (like during breakfast) and laying it open on a table has worked the best for me. I don't need to add stuff to my calendar every day but looking at it every day helps me to get a better idea of what lies ahead. On days where I have nothing to add to my planner, I write a 5 minute journal entry on that page instead.

Other questions to reflect on to make using a paper planner easier:

What do you enjoy about making plans? How can you add that to your planner?

How can you make your planning environment more peaceful? What do you enjoy when it comes to planning?

When I used traditional planners (pre-printed planners, not self-made planners like the Bullet Journal), I tried to find planners that wouldn't punish me much for skipping a day. Dateless planners are ideal.

Pre-dated daily planners (Planners with a whole page dedicated to one day) can cause guilt for skipping a day because of the blank pages. Dated planners with a weekly layout cause less guilt because skipping a day doesn't mean skipping an entire page.

Also with paper planners and calendars, be ready to correct. Use pencil, erasable pen, or whiteout tape to make changes. Having scribbles everywhere can add to feelings of chaos.

What About Digital Calendars?

Digital calendars have the advantage of being able to set reminders. I've found that it's important to be aware of what works for me.

Digital calendars may get a lot of praise, but I tend to forget events if they are stored in my phone. Using a white board instead to remind me of events has worked better. If digital reminders don't do much for you, give paper and other analog methods a try.

Regardless of what type of calendar I choose, I try my best to stick to using only one calendar. There's nothing worse than having some stuff written in my paper planner and then having other things in my digital calendar and then missing something because both don't have the same information.

I used to have a separate calendar for my job, but I decided to merge all that information together. As a result, I have a more realistic view of my day.

Which Calendar is the Best for Me?

Wall calendars, paper planners, digital calendars...with so many choices, it can be difficult to figure out what works. Instead of going by what's popular or what everyone is doing, I've found it's more effective to reflect on ways I've interacted with planning in the past. The best planning method is already within you.

Answer the following questions to get some direction on which methods could be best for you:

1. Do phone reminders always work for you, or do you remember things better when you write them?
2. Do you need portability, or is it okay if you leave your calendar at home most of the time?
3. Do you need to have your calendar with you all the time for reference, or would it be okay if you jot down little things while on the go, and copy them to your calendar when you return home?
4. Is there anything you need to have constantly visible and in your face, so you won't forget about it? What do you need to keep in front of you?
5. If you need visibility, how can you make your calendar visible?

6. If you need portability, how can you make your calendar
    portable?

In this list of questions, **question #1** is the most important. It helps you
to see where your strengths are.

If you forget and ignore phone reminders, rarely check calendar/to-do
apps, or if checking calendar/to-do apps feels like a chore, then you
would want to use analog methods to plan. White boards, paper
planners, and anything else that's part of the physical world. If you are
a person who checks their digital calendar religiously, then digital
solutions won't be a struggle. With your preferences in mind, you can
give more useful answers to questions 5 and 6.

If you've discovered that you need portability and visibility, but you don't
know where to start, below are some suggestions:

Portability

- Use a calendar app for your phone or consider using a small
paper planner.

- Consider if it's easier to take out a pen and write while on
the go or type on your phone.

- When you're not at home, do you spend most of the day
sitting or on your feet? Using a paper planner would be easier
if you're sitting instead of adding things to it while you're
walking around in the middle of shopping or doing other
activities.

- If you prefer writing but would rather not take your paper
planner with you, could you scan parts of it with your phone

to take with you? Or maybe hand copy parts of it into a small notebook?

• If you need almost everything on you all the time, consider using only digital solutions. Bullet Journaling is a good match if you're an analog person.

.

Visibility

• Go for white boards, bulletin boards, and sticky notes (but put all of those sticky notes on a common board so they're not all over the place) to keep information in your face.

• If you prefer paper, use the largest planner you can find and lay it out open on a table.

• Really, laying ANY paper planner opened on a table is useful.

• Use different colors, drawings, or stickers to make important items stand out.

• To add visibility to digital methods, use reminders, widgets, or an app that can pin notes to the notifications bar of your phone.

• To add visibility to a portable sized paper planner or notebook, go for one that's spiral or discbound so you can always have the tasks for the day in your face when you pull it out. Or write your tasks for the day on a sticky note and attach it to the front with a binder clip. Also try using tabs or page markers for sections that you want to get to quickly.

Mixing & Matching

As you try to figure out what fits you, keep in mind that digital methods can be mixed with analog ones. For example, you may prefer a digital calendar to keep track of events but use a white board to keep the most important events visible. Let your imagination run with it and be aware of your needs.

Using a paper calendar but need digital event reminders? Try using your paper calendar as your main calendar, but use note taking apps with a reminders option (Evernote or Google Keep are good examples).

Using a large wall calendar at home but needing a way to jot down events on the go? Try to add events to a portable list, and then copy them to your calendar once you're back at home (You may want to check out the section on ubiquitous capture in the next chapter).

Have a calendar on the wall at home, but want to be able to glance at your calendar while on the go? Take a picture of it with your phone every time you add something to it.

Here's how mixing and matching has worked in my life:

When I was using a Bullet Journal, it had most of my information in one place, and I would leave it open on a table. I inserted colorful tabs to mark pages of information that I regularly referenced, and that was super helpful. I used the tabs more often to find information than the index. However, I rarely carried my Bullet Journal with me. It was usually at home.

Although I no longer use a Bullet Journal, I still write shopping lists and time sensitive items on a white board to keep those things more visible. I take a picture of my shopping lists with my phone so I can have them with me.

While out and about, I use the Workflowy app on my phone to make notes quickly, and I copy that information to my planner once I get back home.

It will take some patience and experimentation to get it right, but when you know what you need, it's easier to find what works.

So, if you're not currently using a calendar, go ahead and get one, and see how it works for you. Add to it all upcoming events, tasks that have specific due dates, and activities that you want to do on specific days.

If you don't feel like running out to buy a planner, check out the list of free planners in the Resource section. If you are more digitally inclined, recommended apps are included there as well.

Managing Tasks

Have you ever felt completely overwhelmed by having a to-do list? In the past I was overcome with anxiety just from looking at my to-do list. There was so much stuff on it, and I felt like it all needed to be done immediately.

Nowadays, I use my monthly calendar the most. Focusing on the main, time sensitive events for each day allows for the most flexibility. When unexpected things happen, only the main events need to be rescheduled. More stress is caused when I have a detailed schedule or a long list of what I should be doing because one little change throws off everything.

However, sometimes I think of tasks that don't have a specific date but need to be done. Often these items repeat themselves over and over in my mind, causing anxiety due to the fear that I might forget about them. In order to reduce the mental load of tasks like these, I've found that it's best to write them down using ubiquitous capture paired with a reminders list.

Step 2: Take Note of Your Day

Taking note of your day with ubiquitous capture answers the question of **what** needs to be addressed.

I cannot believe I'm actually writing good stuff about this. For the longest time, I opposed brainstorming, brain-dumping, or anything related to that. My main reason was that once I started dumping out my ideas, the flow would not stop. My mind created more and more stuff, and I was like, "This is too much for me. I'm better off keeping it all in my head!"

However, my feelings on ubiquitous capture changed when I read the post entitled Minimal ZTD: The Simplest System Possible[1] by Leo Babauta on his blog Zen Habits. The way he presented ubiquitous capture made me realize that this could have a meaningful place in my life. So I gave it another shot.

The first thing that had to change though, was my mindset.

I learned that ubiquitous capture is not for what I need to do today. It is for what I need to do in the future.

Even if I wrote something down that I felt needed to be done today, I would ask myself, "Do I need to do this now?" Usually the answer was no, and I would save it for the future. Sometimes what I thought I needed to do wasn't that important after all. However, if the answer was "Yes, it needs to be done now," I would go ahead and do it instead of writing about it.

This mindset is important because thinking that everything you capture needs to be taken care of right away is overwhelming. But if you approach it like, "What I'm taking note of needs to be done tomorrow or at some point in the future," the stress is reduced significantly. Overall, having a future view is what makes ubiquitous capture work.

The Technique

First, pick a medium.

Your answers to the questions in *Managing Your Day* will help determine how you capture. Consider if analog speaks more to you more than digital or if you need to keep things visible.

---

1. https://zenhabits.net/zen-to-done-ztd-the-ultimate-simple-productivity-system/

Whatever you decide to use for ubiquitous capture needs to be constantly by your side. If you use a Bullet Journal that's easy to carry, your daily spreads would be a good fit for this.

I typically use a small pocket notebook folded over and secured with a binder clip. Not only does the binder clip keep my notebook always open so it's ready to go, but the binder clip is also a great pen holder. I prefer paper, but if I'm in a situation where pen and paper is too awkward (like while shopping), I'll use the my phone to take a note.

By the way, I don't capture tasks only. I also take note of my ideas, thoughts, feelings, observations and all kinds of other stuff.

Second, mark your notes.

I don't usually date my entries, but I could see that being a must have for some people.

If it's a task or idea I really want to keep in mind, I will stick a page marker on that page. Digitally, this could be done by starring the note or changing the color of it.

If I'm taking notes that are related to one subject. I write the name of the subject and draw a single line under it. When I'm done writing about the subject, I draw a line under it at the end to show that I'm done. Then I continue to capture as normal.

This method is similar to one described in the post *How to Use a Simple Pocket Notebook to Improve Your Life*[2] at Lifehacker.

Third, process your notes. And everything else.

---

2. *https://lifehacker.com/how-to-use-a-simple-pocket-notebook-to-improve-your-lif-1713132898*

At the end of the day or at the end of the week, gather all of your notes. Sometimes notes don't make it into the notebook or app that you use for capturing, and they end up on sticky notes or napkins or even in your journal. Collect all of those too.

Then process it all.

Time sensitive tasks go directly to the calendar.

Ideas and notes that I want to hold on to, I type into Workflowy. Try saving these items into a digital or analog note organizing method of your choice.

Some items I've captured have been done already or are no longer relevant, so I cross those out/delete them.

For tasks that are not time sensitive, I add them to my reminders list, which I'll be explaining in the next section.

Once I'm done with processing, I draw two lines under the last line of notes in my notebook. This lets me know where I have stopped processing. I throw out the sticky notes and delete the digital notes that I have no use for anymore.

If you need help with making processing a habit, refer to **Establishing a Routine.**

Step 3: Move Tasks to a Monthly Reminders List

If ubiquitous capture is the "What?," the monthly reminders list is the "When?"

A very lose and non-committal when.

Your first monthly reminders list will be long. But as you copy things over from month to month, it will shrink.

The goal of the reminders list is to keep tasks without a specific due date in one place where they can be easily found. Making it monthly sets a limit on them.

Creating a Monthly Reminders List

Brought down to the very basics, there are a few ways to copy your tasks to a monthly reminders list.

Method 1: A Notebook or Note Page

If you prefer analog methods, you can copy your tasks into a notebook. If you have a planner with a notes section, you could make your list there. If you use a Bullet Journal, a monthly task list is already built into the system.

At the top of your list, write the name of the month. Then under it, list all of the non-time sensitive tasks from your capture method. When the month is over, create a new list with the title of the new month at the top. Then copy tasks from the previous month to the new list.

Method 2: A White Board

With a white board, you may want to divide it in half. On one side, write the name of the current month. Then under that, list all of the non-time sensitive tasks from your capture method. Then at the end of month, create a new list on the other side of the board. Then copy tasks from the previous month to that side.

Using a white board is more visible, but ephemeral. If you want to keep track of previous lists, you may want to take pictures of it each month.

Method 3: A To-Do List or Note-taking App

You will likely choose this if you prefer digital methods. In the app, title your new document or list with the name of the month. Type your non-time sensitive tasks there.

When a new month comes, make a new list, and copy and paste undone items. Then you can either keep the list from the previous month or delete it, whatever you choose.

Shrinking the List

As you copy, you will find that some tasks are not important enough to copy over or don't matter anymore. That is exactly what you want. Over time, my monthly reminders list went from multiple pages to just a half a page thanks to the act of copying things from month to month. Copying makes you question what is important and what you honestly feel like doing.

If you're on the fence about a task, it would be helpful to take a look at your Have and Enjoy lists. Ask yourself: Is this task related to my responsibilities or to something I enjoy? If not, you may want to reconsider why you're copying it to the next month.

If anything on your list becomes time sensitive, immediately move it to your calendar. What is on your calendar is priority. What's on the reminders list is secondary.

Variations

The monthly reminders list is the most basic place to start. As you work with it, notice how you feel. If you have tasks for projects and daily life on the same list and feel like they could be prioritized better, check out Appendix B. If you find that you need more of a weekly list instead of a monthly list, or that you are more motivated by reaching a certain number of completed tasks, check out Appendix C.

And Don't Be Afraid to Be Different

As you try these new methods, you may find that you move between your calendar and reminders list differently from what I've outlined here. And that's okay! Just ask yourself: Is the way I'm doing things working? Am I getting the results (such as more clarity on what to accomplish for the day) that I want? If you are, you're doing it right—even if it doesn't match with what has helped me.

Getting into Action and Feeling Achievement

Usually having a calendar and a reminders list is enough. Persistent tasks without a due date go to the reminders list, and tasks that need to be done soon or have a specific date go to the calendar.

Normally, the calendar holds enough information to see what you need to do for the day.

When I stick to this, I find that I have moments during the day where nothing is planned. So what options are there for the free time?

Something to keep in mind is that as INFPs, what we value is our main motivation. Just the feeling of "getting things done" is not good enough. What we do needs to hinge on our inner values and intentions. Mundane tasks need to either be tied to something valuable or completed with as little effort as possible.

Another thing is that since we're introverted, we go deep into our tasks instead of wide. Having a long list of tasks for the day is for extroverted thinkers. Introverted feelers need only a few tasks to focus on at a time. Having too many tasks can lead to overwhelm.

So, with your free time, you could just do whatever you want! If that's too much freedom, one option is to pull out your reminders list and see what tasks you can take care of during your free moments.

Another alternative is to take note of how you're feeling, how much time you have available, and work along with it. Check out Appendix A, Learning to Work Along with the Way I Feel, for more information on that approach.

Planning Daily Tasks

If you must have a schedule or a separate task list for the day...

- On a piece of paper, white board or whatever you're using, write the day's date at the top.

- First, write any appointments that are on your calendar.

- Then list two or three to-do items.

- Do what you can from the list.

- Take note of how you feel. Imagine your energy level as a battery. Is the battery still in the green, half full, or in the red?

- If you're still feeling energized, add one or two more items to the list and see how you feel after completing them.

- If you're feeling half energized, try adding one five minute task and then take a break.

- If you're feeling like you're in the red, take a break immediately. Take a nap, go for a walk, or do something soothing from your Enjoy list.

And that's it.

The important thing is to add a few tasks to the list at a time, instead of trying to list everything at the start.

Adding items a little at a time allows you to learn how many tasks you can handle. For me, four or five tasks is my limit. Learn how much you can take. Then do less than that.

If you need a better view of how your tasks fit into your day, divide your list for daily tasks into Morning, Afternoon, Evening, or by hours if you dare, before adding the tasks for the day to it.

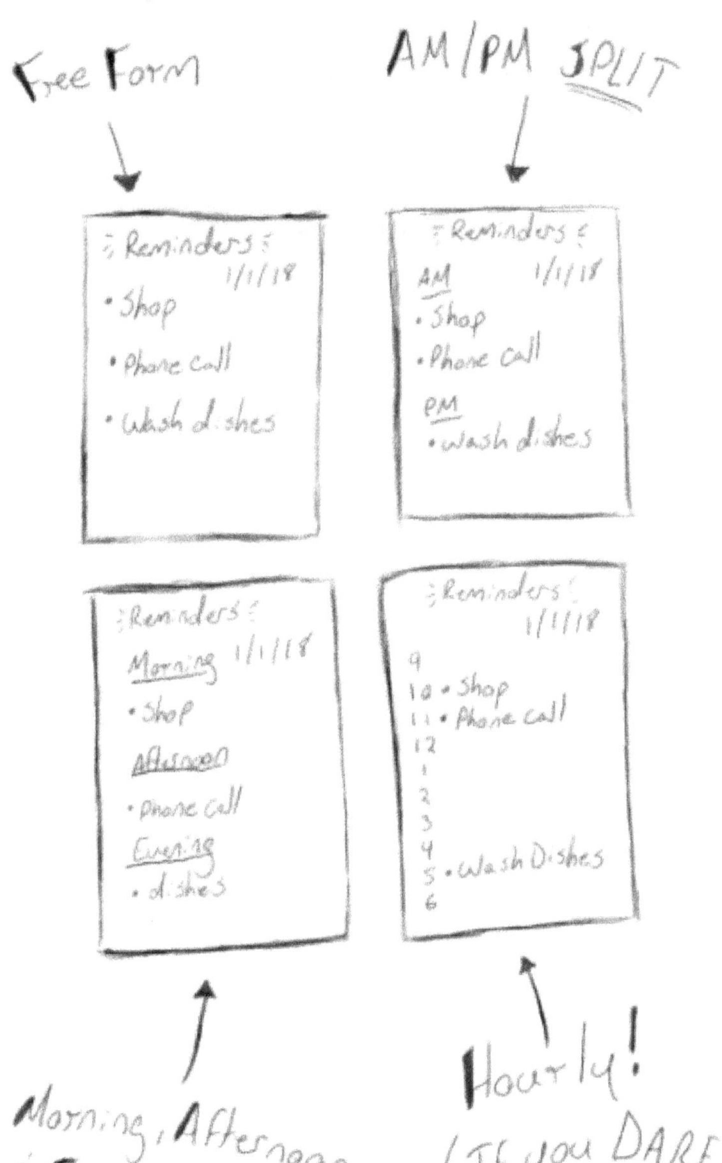

Morning, Afternoon & Evening Schedule

Hourly!
(If you DARE)

But really, try to forego the strict daily to-do list and schedule if possible. Try to create a general sketch of how you want your day to be, not a rigid plan. People who plan by using a calendar tend to be more effective, and strict hourly schedules cramp the creative style of the INFP.

Just as a wide, big picture overview of everything so far—with the tools I've introduced, you can plan using whatever you want.

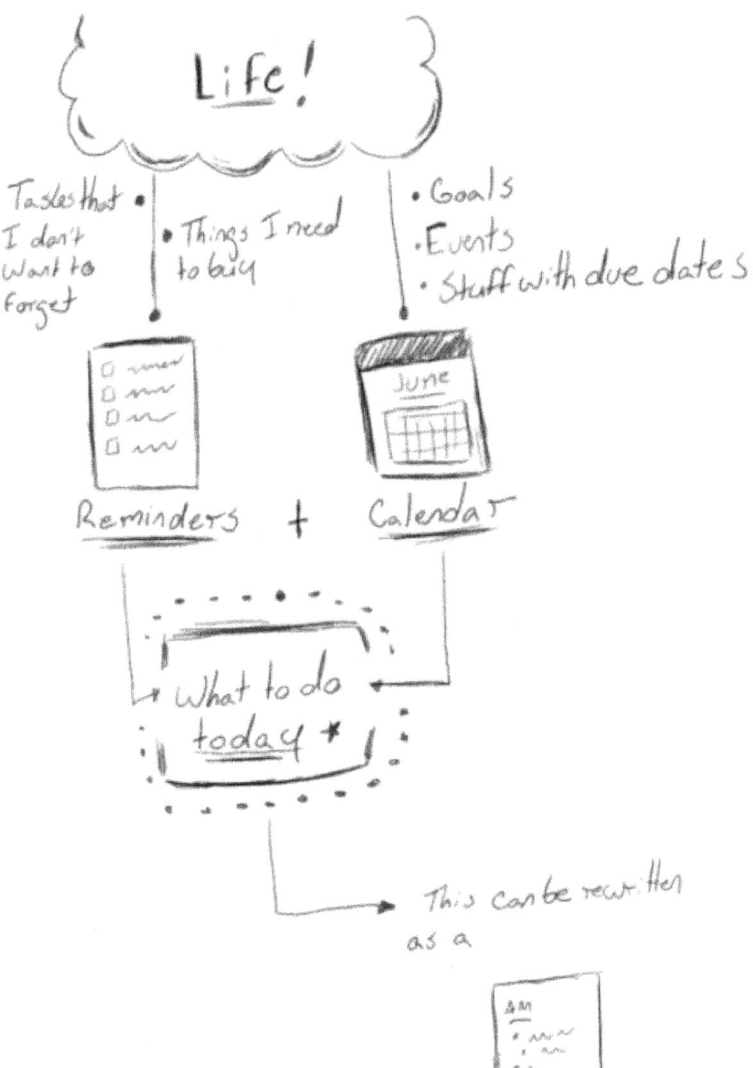
Life!
Tasks that I don't want to forget
Things I need to buy
Goals
Events
Stuff with due dates
Reminders
June
Calendar
+
What to do today *
This can be rewritten as a
AM
PM
Daily Schedule
But this can be optional/as needed.

If you are into traditional journaling, you may want to check out the post on my blog entitled Using Journaling to Transform How You Plan For the Day[1].

Tips for Bullet Journal Users

Before I rolled up my sleeves to create my own planner that fused structure with flexibility (Check out my blog post about my Half-Page Planner[2] for more about that), I used a Bullet Journal. And I really liked it. One of the main parts of the Bullet Journal is the daily spread. This is a good place to rewrite your events for the day so that they are fresh in mind.

Instead of writing a full list of stuff to-do before the day starts, simply focus on the upcoming events. When you do hit a free moment in the day where you're looking for something to do, check your monthly tasks list (This is the BuJo equivalent of a reminders list), copy one task that you think you can get done to your daily spread, and see how far you can get on it.

Don't Be Afraid of Basic

Often when I look at the Bullet Journals others share on Instagram, their daily pages are full of all kinds of things besides a to-do list. There's water tracking and daily gratitude and meal plans. At first, I started out by copying this trend, but I found it discouraging because I couldn't fill out these other elements regularly. I'm doing good enough to keep up with what's going on every day.

To get rid of the guilt, I went back to the basics.

---

1. https://www.arcadiapage.com/2019/07/using-journaling-to-transform-how-you.html

2. https://www.arcadiapage.com/2018/10/free-minimal-half-page-planner.html

When Bullet Journaling, my daily pages were simply the day's date, events/tasks, and notes. If I wanted to add artwork, that was cool, but no more written information than the bare minimum. Other things that I wanted to track like my mood or what I ate, I put on a separate dedicated tracking page. Once I stopped mixing trackers or gratitude journals with my daily pages, I had no more half-used daily pages. Skipping a day doesn't matter because each new entry could go under the last one.

Generally, in Bullet Journaling when things start going wrong, go back to the basics.

And being basic can be beautiful. I recommend checking out minimal.plan[3] and the Lazy Genius Collective[4] for some nice examples of simplicity. Also Bulletjournal.com[5] is the best place to go to refresh yourself on the basics.

The rule of keeping it simple applies to traditional planners as well. I avoid planners with a ton of daily prompts to fill in because they only frustrate me with my inability to keep up.

However, another question arises. **When picking a task from the reminders list, how do you decide what to do?**

Setting Priorities

As an INFP, my priorities change throughout the day. At one point, cleaning may be a priority but that can change into exploring a new idea. I find that when I try to force myself to prioritize, everything feels like it has the same amount of urgency. INFPs take things as they come, from the environment or mentally. This is another reason it's best to add tasks to the day as it goes, instead of mapping out everything from the start.

---

3. http://minimal-plan.com/en/how-to-start-a-bullet-journal/

4. http://www.thelazygeniuscollective.com/blog/how-to-bullet-journal

5. https://bulletjournal.com/

My goal is not to fill my day with stuff to do. My mind can come up with enough stuff to do on its own. The goal is to do what needs to be addressed for the day plus what I want to work on.

With that in mind, I avoid filling my days with only time sensitive tasks if it's not necessary—especially if those are mundane tasks that don't intertwine with my values. It's okay to tackle the mundane things, just don't fill the day with them. For example, doing a day full of cleaning when you crave to do something else. Do you really have to clean the entire day? Or would doing a half day be okay too? Or two hours? Be flexible with yourself and don't be afraid to adjust expectations.

There have been times when I knew friends were coming over, and I spent the entire day cleaning the house before they came. Later I learned that taking an hour or less to clean the bathroom and the kitchen worked just as well, and I enjoyed the company more. Even when things are time sensitive, perfectionism can cause me to add more to the task than necessary. In the end, I try to balance my day between time sensitive items and doing what I feel like.

If your day is packed to max, try rescheduling some activities and making time to recharge instead.

Use Your Feelings

It also helps to know how you want your day to feel. What emotions would you like to feel today?

Knowing the answer can help with setting priorities. For a moment, try to imagine yourself reaching your main intentions for the day in detail. Pay attention to what you see and where you are, down to the colors. Be aware of touch, sound, and taste. Live there for a moment.

Then, write the top three emotions that come to you. What do you already have now in your life that creates those emotions? How can you add more of that to your day?

The Dreaded Overwhelm

No matter how relaxed and balanced you are with your plans, at some point the feeling of overwhelm is going to rear its ugly head. Unexpected things happen, and when they do, sometimes they can overtake us. When I'm faced with overwhelm, I first ask myself:

What can I do today for today?

Not what I can do today for tomorrow or what can I do today for next week. As an INFP, my brain lives in the future, and when I'm overwhelmed, I am often thinking about what I need to do tomorrow for next week, next month, for the next 6 months...it's like the future implodes into one tiny point of time.

Focusing directly on the day ahead and nothing more helps. Once I figure out what I need to do today for today, then I can think about what I can do today for tomorrow—tomorrow being the next day only. When I am overwhelmed, I try to limit my foresight to what is immediately ahead.

Managing a Social Life

If my day is full of socializing, I try to do more relaxing and solitude during my free time. And by solitude, that means avoiding **social media, emails, phone calls and the like**, so that I'll have the energy to enjoy my social engagements.

On the flip side, I've also found it helpful to set specific times on my calendar to contact people. Sometimes I get so lost in my projects that I need to remind myself to reach out to others.

Bringing Tasks into Reality

Although we INFPs like to do what we feel like, our inferior extroverted thinking makes achievement and getting things done attractive to us. However, we are not ESTJs and the forceful, "get it all done now as efficiently as possible!" can backfire. We need more of a gentle push forward. Here are some things I've tried to make progress on my tasks and keep them in front of me.

Timers

Some days I'm really torn between what I want to do and what I have to do, and it's hard for me to set a priority. To make progress in both areas, I set a timer to work on what I want to do for 25 minutes.

Then when time's up, I work on what I have to do for 15 minutes. Then switch to what I want to do for another 25 minutes. I continue to alternate between what I want to do and have to do. I've found this to be very effective, especially when working on projects where it's easy for me to lose myself.

I like using timers to create limits for how long I spend on activities. When I do, I feel like I'm in control of my time. If I run out of time to complete something, I write down the task I need to do next, and then plan to continue my work on another day.

If you don't have the time or motivation to set a 20-minute timer (and unfortunately that does happen) set a 5-minute timer instead and see what you can do. I have been amazed by how many dishes I can wash or how much I can tidy my desk just by taking 5 minutes at a time. Five minutes is definitely better than nothing.

Some projects are very immersive, and in that case, I need more time awareness than management. In those situations I like using an hourly reminder app that tells me what time it is every hour, so I don't lose track of time. Using a clock with a chime can also be helpful.

Keep Due Dates Where You Can See Them

Once again, I have good things to say about the white board. Writing due dates on a white board is a great way for me to keep what I need to do in front of my face.

If you prefer not to use a white board, highlight time sensitive tasks on your calendar or write them in a different color. Set corresponding reminders on your phone.

Also create reminders to check on things that you need to monitor on a regular basis, such as watering plants or changing the oil in your car.

One point about setting reminders: I find that for reoccurring reminders, for the first month or so they work, but then after that, I start ignoring them. Because of that, I set reminders for important one-time events and keep my eye on the calendar for repeating tasks. I'm more likely to do reoccurring tasks if I look on my calendar or whiteboard and see it upcoming, versus getting constant phone reminders. With repetitive phone dreminders, I usually get annoyed, press snooze, and forget about it. Be aware of when phone reminders work for you and when they don't.

Another thing to try: When putting a due date on the calendar, set a due date that is earlier than the real due date. This isn't guaranteed to stop procrastination, but at least you may get an earlier start on the task than usual.

Celebrate Your Half-Done Tasks

Don't leave half-done tasks for the day unmarked. Making progress on tasks is just as important as finishing them. If you have check-boxes on your list, fill it in half-way. One method that I like is marking half-done tasks as done and then rewriting them for the next day.

For example, on a Monday I could have "Write blog post." I write half of it and mark the task as done. Then for the next day I make a task called, "Write more of my blog post." As I go about this one step at a time, eventually that post is done.

This also works well for tasks that I don't feel like doing. It allows me to take things one step at a time and feel like each step matters.

Reflect on the Day

As INFPs, our days often don't go as planned. However, that's not a bad thing. What makes it feel not so great is that we have a hard time seeing what we have accomplished throughout the day. If you stuck to your plans or not, take some time to reflect on what you did and appreciated about your day. I find that writing what I accomplished for the day makes me aware of all the things I did versus all the things I didn't do, and I feel more satisfied.

Think about the following questions:

• What did I complete today?

• What do I like the most about what I accomplished today?

• What is one thing that I can do in ten minutes or less to make tomorrow a little better?

Writing down a few things to be grateful for can also help you to reflect on the little ways that your day was meaningful, even if it didn't feel like it.

Conclusion

I hope I've helped you to find some direction as you discover how to use your time more effectively to reach your goals.

And I know I mentioned this at the start but please remember to...

Do What Works

If some advice here has been helpful and made a difference, that's great! If you have your own personal method that works well, that's great too. Just don't change what is already effective because I've shared something different. Also, don't be afraid to tailor these techniques to fit better with the way you see the world.

For more articles about INFPs, emotional health, and my other creative pursuits, check out my blog at www.arcadiapage.com and feel free to message me on Twitter @arcadiapage.

Appendix A: Learning to Work Along with the Way I Feel

One of the ideas I've come across often when reading articles about doing creative work is the concept of working with your natural energy flow throughout the day. There are times during the day when it's easier to accomplish creative tasks than others.

For me that has been a difficult thing to nail down. Sometimes I feel like working on things in the morning. Other times I don't. When and what I feel like working on constantly shifts, so I've always felt that working along with the way I feel is a totally unrealistic idea.

But then I came across *Sketch Now, Think Later* by Mike Yoshiaki Daikubara. I started reading his book mainly for the real-life sketching advice, and it is one of the best books on sketching that I've read, especially when it comes to making art on the go in a short amount of time.

However, what also amazed me is how Daikubara looks at time. He explained that he's found that moments throughout his day typically fall into one of four categories:

- Little Time/Lots of Energy
- Lots of Time/Little Energy
- Lots of Time/Lots of Energy
- Little Time/Little Energy

Then he mentioned what he does for each category:

- Little Time/Lots of Energy: This is when he sketches the most.
- Lots of Time/Little Energy: He goes out for a walk.
- Lots of Time/Lots of Energy: Sometimes he creates sketches,

but he often feels lost in all the possibilities due to the excess amount of time.

- Little Time/Little Energy: Rest.

Feeling totally inspired, I decided to take this mindset a step further. I created a list of activities I could do for each category.

For example, for the **Lots of Time/Lots of Energy** category, I made a list kind of like this:

Household

- Cook for the week.
- Do deep cleaning.

Projects

- Write multiple blog posts.
- Draw comic pages.
- Writing: Planning and plotting new stories.

Fun/Social

- Go on a social outing.
- Read a How-To book.

My real list is a bit longer, but this is basically how it is. Since the category is **Lots of Time/Lots of Energy**, I focused on how I would spend the day if I had all the time to do what I wanted. In reality, this mainly applies to vacation days and days where I decide to cancel everything and do what I want.

Typically, my day falls into **Little Time/Lots of Energy**. For that, my list is like this:

Household

- Break chores into 5 or 10-minute tasks.
- Make simple to cook meals.
- Shop online or go to just one store to get everything I need.

Projects

- Writing: Write in stream of consciousness. No backspacing. Use a Pomodoro timer. When editing, only edit for typos, punctuation, or to add extra info.
- Comic making: Draw characters on pages. Exclude hands. Erase minimally.

Fun/Social

- Short social media check-ins.
- Send a text.
- Make a short phone call.

Here I've listed the same activities as the previous list, except the activities are condensed so they can be done in less time. Under chores I break up large tasks into smaller ones. For my projects, I take a "work fast now, perfect later" approach. At moments like this, I don't have time to be a perfectionist. The best I can do is get everything out and improve on it later. This method isn't ideal for all projects, but for me it works with writing and art.

Also, I've created portable kits for each of my projects that are focused on keeping my tools simple and to a minimum. I can work on writing projects and post to my blog where ever I am by using phone apps. Since I'm an artist, I also keep a makeup bag in my purse with a pen, sketchbook, and a watercolors kit. Having little project kits like this is even great for when I'm at home because the setup time is reduced. Overall, this category takes the most creativity because it involves figuring out more efficient ways of doing things.

The next category I find myself in the most often is **Lots of Time/Little Energy**. My list is like this:

Household

- Easy, one-minute chores or chores that I can do while sitting.
- Take care of plants.
- Buy pre-made food for dinner.
- Shop on-line.

Easy Project Tasks

- Finish a sketch. Add notes and color.
- Add color/tone/or speech bubbles to comics.
- Edit fiction/non-fiction/blog posts. Edit for details, style, and overall story flow.

Relaxing

- Go for a walk.
- Power nap.
- Pilates.
- Cup of tea. Something fruity or spicy.
- Casual reading.
- Journal.
- Watch a movie or TV show.

When I have little energy, that's a cue some self-care is in order. I avoid tasks that require my unwavering attention. Since I'm an introvert, I reduce my social activities, so I don't become more drained. Also, when it comes to projects, I've found that this is when my mind is most ready to focus on the details. Now I can perfect what I made in **the Little Time/ Lots of Energy** category. Also, when I'm in this category, I try to pay attention to when my mood changes. Usually at some point during the day, I return to **Little Time/Lots of Energy**.

The last category is **Little Time/Little Energy**, and when I find myself here, the most effective thing I can do is take a short nap. I'm not fit to do anything else. Even if I try to stay awake by doing relaxing breathing exercises, I fall asleep anyways.

I shift through categories throughout the day, and I've found that thanks to this method, I am more aware of my limits. In the past I would push myself too hard to work on things, even when I knew I had little energy. Now, I'm better able to check in with myself, which is nice because that frazzled, over the edge feeling is not so great.

Appendix B: Introduction to the Matrix Style Reminders List & Project Planning

One of the hardest things for me to learn was how to put my daily tasks together with my project tasks without getting overwhelmed. So here I'm showing one method I used to revamp my reminders list, so I could better manage personal projects.

Important Notes:

- Hold off from trying this style of reminders list until you are comfortable with the basic reminders list.

- You may find this method to be either a breath of fresh air or more complicated. Be aware of your feelings as you read over the instructions. If you feel unease, this method may not be for you (You may want to check out Appendix C: Creating a Weekly Reminder's List as an alternative). Always do what comes the easiest.

Inspiration for this technique comes from the Eisenhower Matrix, the IKE app, and the book *How to Be Everything* by Emilie Wapnick.

First, let's remake your reminders list. On a piece of paper, whiteboard, or whatever medium you are using for your reminders list, draw a 2x2 matrix. If you're using a digital device try using an app that allows you to make four separate categories or use the IKE app if you have Android.

When I used a Bullet Journal, I created this list to replace my "monthly tasks" spread. Even if you don't use a Bullet Journal, I've noticed that this method works well if it's made with the current month in mind and throughout the month you try to complete what's on it. There are four different sections: **Focus, Goals, Fit In**, and **Back-Burner**.

Look at your reminders list and sort your tasks, writing them in the section they fit in.

The **Focus** section is for tasks that I am aching to get done and projects that I'm currently working on or have a strong drive to work on.

The **Goals** section is for things that I want to achieve for the month (for example, exercising 10 minutes a day).

The **Fit In** section is for all the little things that need to get done but can be squeezed in after my focus tasks. They're important, but not THAT important. These tasks can be taken care of whenever I have free time.

The **Back-Burner** section is for tasks that there isn't an urgent need for me to get to.

Adding Projects to the Matrix Reminders List

1. **Write another list with two categories: Focus Projects and Wishlist Projects.** Focus Projects are the projects that you are working on now or really have a desire to get started on. Wishlist Projects are projects that you would like to start in the future or are currently working on a little bit here and there with very little urgency. Keep your list of Focus Projects down to 1 to 3 items. With Wishlist Projects, list as many as you want.

2. **Copy your Focus Projects to the Focus section of your revamped reminders list.** Also, look at the tasks in your other squares. If any of them are related to your Focus Projects, move those tasks to the Focus section as well.

3. **Now let's look at your Wishlist Projects.** Choose one or two of those projects you would like to take on for the month and copy them to the Back-Burner section of your new Reminders List. As the month progresses, add any new projects that pop

into your mind to your Wishlist.

Sometimes Projects and Goals intercept each other. For example, this month I may have the goal of working on my novel at least 30 minutes a day. If I have a project that is also my goal for the month, I tend to feel better moving it to the Focus section because it's something I really want to pay attention to. Just be aware of how you view things and go with how you feel when it comes to which activities go where.

You can still add tasks that keep repeating themselves in your head to this list, except now you have meaningful categories to put them in. Plus, you can see the main projects that you want to work on for the month. And as usual, copy items with due dates to the calendar.

Okay, so how does this fit in with everything?

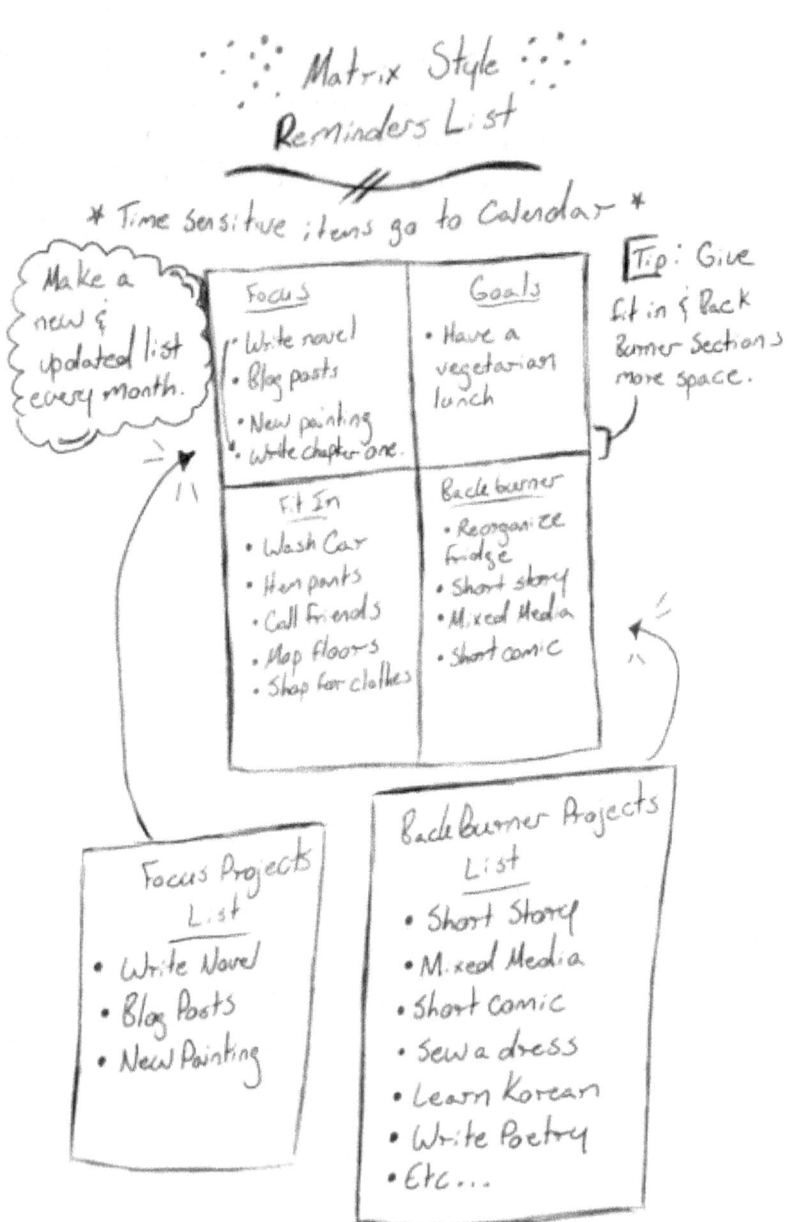
Matrix Style
Reminders List

* Time Sensitive items go to Calendar *

Make a new & updated list every month.

Tip: Give Fit in & Back Burner Sections more space.

Focus
• Write novel
• Blog posts
• New painting
• Write chapter one.

Goals
• Have a vegetarian lunch

Fit In
• Wash Car
• Hem pants
• Call friends
• Mop floors
• Shop for clothes

Back burner
• Reorganize fridge
• Short story
• Mixed Media
• Short comic

Focus Projects List
• Write Novel
• Blog Posts
• New Painting

Back Burner Projects List
• Short Story
• Mixed Media
• Short Comic
• Sew a dress
• Learn Korean
• Write Poetry
• Etc...

Imagine that it's time for you to look at your planner. First you check out your monthly calendar. There are no events or tasks scheduled for the day. Nice! So now what? Then you pull out your new reminders list. You could start your day by taking on a project from the **Focus** section or try to get things done by working on what's in the **Fit In** section. You could also spend some time working towards something in the **Goals** section.

But what about those projects in the **Back-Burner** section?

As often as you can, set aside some "tinkering time" (This is a term I've borrowed from *How to Be Everything* by Emilie Wapnick) —that is, time to play around with your Back-Burner projects. I like to set a timer for 30 to 40 minutes and then dabble in something from my list. I try to spend a little time with my Back-Burner projects a few times a week, while giving most of my attention to my Focus projects. If you don't have that much time, there's nothing wrong with giving only 10 to 15 minutes to a project. However, if push comes to shove, and you have to decide between dabbling or working on a Focus project, try to pick a Focus project.

My favorite thing about "tinkering time" is that it's also a great way to take a break from my Focus projects if I've been spending a lot of time on them.

At the end of the month make a new matrix style reminders list, copying over what's not been done to the list for the new month.

Method Variations to Try

Matrix + Reminders

The matrix style reminders list could be used to simply create an overview of what you would like to accomplish for the month. Then the monthly reminders list can be used for tasks that you come across as you go about your daily life.

Projects Only

The matrix style reminders list could be used for projects and goals only. Other reminders could be saved on a monthly reminders list.

Regardless of what you try, remember that the *calendar is king*. Tasks that have due dates should be migrated to your calendar.

Dealing with Overwhelm & Underwhelm

If looking at your Focus Projects makes your heart race or if you try to stick to it and can't keep up, you may need to reduce the number of projects in that section. Move some of them to the Back-Burner section and give them attention during your tinkering time.

My Projects Wishlist is a long one, but even so, there are projects that I'm more excited to get to than others. I put hearts next to the projects that I can't wait to get to the most, so that when I do have tinkering time, I know what I want to do. If you have a long Wishlist, try putting notations next to your favorite projects so that it's easier to pick what to work on.

On the other end of the spectrum is boredom. If you feel bored or if there is a certain Back Burner project that you're not making as much progress on as you would like, move it to the Focus section.

Overall, don't be afraid to move projects from the Back-Burner section to the Focus section or the other way around. Doing so is how you can learn what kind of activity load you can handle.

Experiment and see what works.

For more about balancing your projects, I recommend reading *How to Be Everything* by Emilie Wapnick. What she shared has helped me to create a system that allows me to manage my daily tasks and projects in a way that makes sense.

If you're looking for a more gamified and analytical way of managing projects and tasks on your reminders list on a weekly basis, see the next section.

Appendix C: Creating a Weekly Reminders List

Having a monthly reminders list served me well for a long time. But then my life changed. I became busier. My daily schedule became hectic and erratic. On top of that, more new and exciting hobbies started to catch my eye. So not only was my outer life unpredictable but what I wanted to do became more unpredictable as well. My monthly reminders list could not handle all the instability, and it grew super long and unmanageable.

What brought things back to order was creating a structured weekly reminders list. Here's how to make one. You can use whatever you like, but I like using Workflowy for my list. In fact, it was an article on the Workflowy blog[1] that introduced me to this method.

This method is also great for seeing how much of a project you can work on week by week when you have a schedule that's all over the place.

1. **Write down your goals for the week.** What would you like to accomplish next week? What would you like to get done? Write one chapter of a novel? Deep clean your bedroom?
2. **Under each weekly goal, write the steps needed to accomplish it.** Keep the steps small. For example, if my goal is to clean the house, steps can be: vacuum the floors, wash dishes, dust, etc... Break down big goals into small parts.
3. **For each of the smaller steps, assign either a 1, 2, 3, or 5.**

I assign a **1** to a task if I can do it with very little effort and time, and I know exactly what needs to be done.

I assign a **2** to a task that takes a little more time (10 minutes or more) and I know what needs to be done.

---

1. https://blog.workflowy.com/2018/10/04/sprints/

I assign a **3** to a task that will take a while (over 30 minutes), and that I may or may not know how to get done.

I assign a **5** to a task that will take a long time (hours), or that I have no idea of how long it will take to complete. I also assign a 5 to tasks that I don't know how to start and will have to do extra research to figure out. I can then break it down into smaller, simpler tasks. This is great for projects. (As far as why I use the numbers 1, 2, 3, and 5, check out the article "Individual Sprints" on the Workflowy blog[2])

1. **At the top of the list, write the date of the week and:** *Estimation=25, Actual=0.*
2. **Add up the numbers for ALL the tasks on your list.** If the sum of your tasks is more than 25, highlight, bold, or put a star next to the tasks you want to get done the most until the total of those tasks add up to 25. Those are priority tasks.
3. **Go about your week, using the weekly task list as your guide.** See how much you can get done. You can keep track of your progress by adding up the completed items and writing the total after "Actual =."
4. **At the end of the week, add up all your points.** If you got way less than 25, you may want to lower your estimation for the next week, so your task list can better reflect how you actually use your time. If you went 10 points or more over 25, you may want to up your estimation by a few points for the next week. Adjust your estimated points for the next week by looking at how you did the previous week.

With this method, as the weeks go by, you can get a clear picture of how much you can and can't accomplish in a week. Sometimes during the week, I think of other things that I want to do that won't fit into the

---

2. https://blog.workflowy.com/2018/10/04/sprints/

current week. So, I keep a separate "Wishlist" of future tasks, so when the time comes for me to make a new weekly reminder's list, I can plan to take care of those items if I want to.

I also make sure to copy time sensitive weekly tasks and tasks that I want to do on a specific day to the calendar.

Recommended Resources

Free Planners

Canva.com[1]

Bulletjournal.com[2]

Pocketmod.com[3]

Planner Printables from my blog, www.arcadiapage.com[4]

Other Planners to Consider

Hobonichi Techo[5]

The Simplified Planner by Emily Ley[6]

JSTORY Medium Personal Wide Spaces Undated Monthly Planner (available at various online retailers)

Simple Digital Planning Apps & Methods

A note on apps: With digital applications, it's best to stick to one or two apps and learn them VERY well. You will find that when you learn how to use all of the features in an app effectively, you will be more productive.

---

1. http://www.canva.com

2. http://www.bulletjournal.com

3. https://pocketmod.com/

4. https://www.arcadiapage.com/2018/10/free-minimal-half-page-planner.html

5. https://www.1101.com/store/techo/en/

6. https://www.emilyley.com/collections/simplified-planner

Workflowy[7] (I highly recommend reading up on the tips and tricks in the Workflowy blog[8] as well to get the most out of this app)

Todoist[9]

Tape[10] by Aeriform (Desktop Only)

Plain Text Planning Method:

- Getting Started: What's the Bare Minimum You Need to Be Productive with Plain Text?[11] – The Plain Text Project

- Plain Text Planning Template (Just copy & paste) https://github.com/jukil/plain-text-life

- How to Create a Calendar in Plain Text: A Plain Text Personal Organizer - Daniel Lucraft[12]

- Organizing Plain Text Files: Strategies for Naming Your Text Files[13]

Plain Text Planning Apps:

Journee[14] (Desktop Only)

Typora[15] (Desktop Only)

---

7. http://www.workflowy.com

8. https://blog.workflowy.com/

9. http://www.todoist.com

10. https://aeriform.itch.io/tape

11. https://scottnesbitt.gitlab.io/2019/03/19/productive.html

12. http://danlucraft.com/blog/2008/04/plain-text-organizer/

13. https://scottnesbitt.gitlab.io/2017/08/15/naming.html

14. https://adueck.github.io/journee/

15. https://typora.io/

Jotterpad[16] (Android and iOS Only)

iA Writer[17]

Thinking Visually

Mind Mapping: mind42.com[18]

Mind maps from Mind 42 can be exported to work in Freeplane[19].

Visual Notes: How to Take Sketch Notes from Jetpens.com[20]

Books to Read

Design the Life You Love. Birsel, Ayse. Potter/Ten Speed/Harmony/
Rodale.

*Was That Really Me?: How Everyday Stress Brings Out Our Hidden
Personality.* Quenk, Naomi. Quercus.

The Comprehensive INFP Survival Guide. Priebe, Heidi. Thought
Catalog Books.

One Small Step Can Change Your Life: The Kaizen Way. Maurer, Robert.
Workman Publishing Company.

How to Be Everything. Wapnick, Emilie. HarperOne.

Sustainable Creativity. Nobbs, Micheal. https://www.gogently.co/ (This
one is free!)

---

16. https://2appstudio.com/jotterpad/

17. https://ia.net/writer

18. https://mind42.com/

19. https://sourceforge.net/projects/freeplane/

20. https://www.jetpens.com/blog/sketchnotes-a-guide-to-visual-note-taking/pt/892

Work Simply: Embracing the Power of Your Personal Productivity Style.
Tate, Carson. Penguin Group (USA) LLC.

Don't miss out!

Visit the website below and you can sign up to receive emails whenever Arcadia Page publishes a new book. There's no charge and no obligation.

https://books2read.com/r/B-A-XZED-GVUW

BOOKS 2 READ

Connecting independent readers to independent writers.

Also by Arcadia Page

Idealist Dreams: How I Learned to Plan as an INFP
I Want to Do All the Things: Finding Balance as a Polymath,
Multipotentialite & Renaissance Soul
I Can't Help Being an INFP Writer
The Little Book of Tiny Tasks: Make Your Life More Calm While
Getting Things Done 5 Minutes at a Time
Thoughtful Planning: How I Learned to Use Journaling to Set
Intentional Goals & Design Flexible Days

Watch for more at www.arcadiapage.com.

About the Author

Arcadia Page is a writer and artist from central Florida. When she's not writing, she enjoys drawing, reading, and crafting. She shares her life with her husband, who also enjoys writing stories.

Read more at www.arcadiapage.com.

9 798201 549053